P9-AZW-141

Country Living

Decorating STYLE

The New Look of Country

Text by
RHODA MURPHY

Foreword by
NANCY MERNIT SORIANO

Hearst Books ▪ NEW YORK

Copyright © 1999 by Hearst
Communications, Inc.

All rights reserved. No part of this book may
be reproduced or utilized in any form or by
any means, electronic or mechanical, including photocopying, recording, or by any infor-
mation storage or retrieval system, without
permission in writing from the Publisher.
Inquiries should be addressed to Permissions
Department, William Morrow and Company,
Inc., 1350 Avenue of the Americas, New
York, N.Y. 10019.

It is the policy of William Morrow and
Company, Inc., and its imprints and affiliates,
recognizing the importance of preserving
what has been written, to print the books we
publish on acid-free paper, and we exert our
best efforts to that end.

Library of Congress Cataloging-in-
Publication Data
Murphy, Rhoda Jaffin.
    Country living decorative style / by
Rhoda Murphy and the editors of
Country living.
        p. cm.
    ISBN 0-688-16752-7
    1. Interior decoration—United States—
History—20th century. 2. Decoration
and ornament, Rustic—United States.
I. Country living (New York, N.Y.) II. Title.
NK2004.M8697 1999
747—dc21
                            99-42886
                                CIP

Printed in Singapore

First Edition

10 9 8 7 6 5 4 3 2 1

For Country Living:
Nancy Mernit Soriano
Editor-in-Chief

www.williammorrow.com
www.countryliving.com

Produced by Smallwood & Stewart, Inc.,
New York City

Designer ■ Susi Oberhelman
Editor ■ Maria Menechella

CONTENTS

FOREWORD

MORE THAN A DECADE AGO, we published a book called *Country Living Country Decorating*, a comprehensive look at country style in America. It was an ambitious undertaking, one that we felt would stand the test of time. And it has—to this day, the book continues to sell across the country.

But the meaning—and the look—of country has continued to evolve in the years since we first published *Country Decorating* (and in the 20 years since the launch of *Country Living* magazine). As a decorating style it has become even more encompassing, mixing old with new, formal with informal, and period styles with flea market finds. It continues to honor the past—but with a new vitality and spirit that makes *Country Decorating* the perfect complement to today's lifestyle. It is a look that can be simple and sophisticated, rustic and retro, but always comfortable and inviting—a look that is truly American.

What follows on these pages is a celebration of country style today: of old buildings lovingly restored; new houses mindful of the past, and rooms that speak volumes about individual expression and the universal appeal of the country lifestyle. We've taken a new look at the Capes, saltboxes, cabins, and barns that we love, and explored the rooms that make them classic and so much a part of our national character.

We hope you will find inspiration here, as well as renewed enthusiasm for what we believe to be the best of American country today.

NANCY MERNIT SORIANO
Editor-in-Chief

A Hou

se in the COUNTRY

AMERICAN COUNTRY HAS MANY faces, shaped by different periods, places, and people. Our heritage encompasses such diverse elements as the elegant Federal-style row-houses of Eastern cities like Philadelphia and Boston, the log-dwellings of early Midwestern settlers, and the adobe structures of the Southwest. Regional architectural and decorating differences were—and to an extent still are—dictated by climate, light, and terrain. The brilliant desert weather of the Southwest, for instance, requires a different design approach than the more muted sunlight and changing seasons of New England. Some homeowners choose to follow the spirit of their house when decorating, others enjoy mixing regional themes. It is this decorating freedom that gives American country its broad appeal and defines American country style—to put it simply, there's something in it for everyone. ■

American

VERNACUL

I. Per

The NORTHEAST

DESIGN IN THE NORTHEAST is shaped by the history of the area. The homes here range from a rustic cottage on Maine's rocky coast, to an elegant brownstone in New York City, to an old farmhouse in the hills of Pennsylvania. Although the settings differ, the mission of the homeowners is the same—to fill their homes with objects they love. As one homeowner puts it: "We didn't have a big decorating budget, but that was all right because we just wanted the place to make us smile."

A boys-camp bunkhouse became a cute summer cottage thanks to a husband and wife who overhauled it and filled it with painted furniture and cheerful textiles. Foul-weather gear is always ready by the front door in a lift-top bench (opposite). A grain-painted navigational box from the early 1800s rests on top. A trip to Sweden inspired the owners to paint the doors yellow and the floors white, and to place a green cupboard in the living room (above left). Open shelving and painted beadboard cabinets with playful fish pulls lend charm to the tiny kitchen (above right).

A sophisticated country style looks quite at home in a one-bedroom apartment in Brooklyn. The owner started with a few dramatic pieces of dark cherry furniture, then added color and pattern. The dining room pedestal table is one of those cherry pieces (above). Checks on one set of chairs and solids on another keep the pattern from looking too busy. The dining area's hanging rack was custom-built from fiberboard, an engineered-wood product. Even a small room can handle an oversized piece of furniture. In the living room (right), a massive armoire anchors the space and serves as a much-needed focal point. The dining room chairs can easily be moved in here when extra seating is needed.

A steady style and similar colors are a must in a small space, especially an apartment. To give their 1949 apartment in New York City a fresh look, a couple turned to yellow walls and textured fabrics. Complementary colors and patterns pull the living area together (top left). Linen curtains edged with gold echo the sofa's tones and the pale lemon of the walls. Lampshades that resemble pouffy hats pick up the chairs' striped motif. The owners highlighted the green wallpaper in the bedroom (bottom left) with green accents such as the chair in the corner (a flea-market find), the glass lamp by the bed, and a collection of art pottery.

A quilt expert turned her Manhattan flat into a calm backdrop for her handiwork. A wool Victorian variation quilt claims attention in the living room (opposite top left). On the other side of the room, a circa 1910 white-on-red Flying Geese variation hangs. Several antiques from the owner's home state of Kentucky—including the late 1800s hanging cupboard—populate the entry hall (opposite top right). Large baskets beneath a farm table (opposite bottom) provide storage space for the owner's quilts and allow her to change her wall art at will.

Tucked away in the rolling meadows of eastern Pennsylvania, a 1700s fieldstone farmhouse was transformed into the Auldridge Mead Inn. Period pieces and old paint treatments bring 18th-century flavor to the historic house. A pair of Shaker-made children's chairs from the late 1800s and a set of old ice skates appear as sculpture when hung from a peg rail in one of the guest rooms (above). A small-scale horse-and-heart stencil rings the room. Craftsman Craig Mattoli (who owns the inn along with master chef Karyn Coigne) sponge-painted the mantel and doorway of a guest room (right) then coated them with a dark-red oil glaze. At the foot of the 19th-century mahogany spool bed sits an impressive Sheraton-style Maryland blanket chest dating to the early 1800s.

The MIDWEST

STRADDLED BY THE two coasts, the Midwest takes its cues from both. From the East there is a love of fine-lined pieces and patterns and Victoriana (the period when much of the Midwest was settled), while from the West comes a preference for rugged pioneer pieces and a pristine backdrop of whites. These homes run the architectural gamut, from an updated Illinois farmhouse, to a new home in a suburban housing development, to an ornate Italianate mansion in Ohio. The owners—all inveterate collectors—rely on intriguing objects to bring character to their homes.

A rtwork takes on three dimensions in an Illinois collector's renovated farmhouse. In the living room (opposite), each piece was carefully chosen for its texture and patina, including an arrow weathervane and a salvaged fanlight transom. A guest room (above left), christened the green room for its verdant touches, features an architectural fragment with cutout stars hanging above a mid-19th-century rope bed. Pillows made from worn-out wool blankets support an Amish doll in another guest room (above right). A salvaged "eyebrow" screen accents the wall.

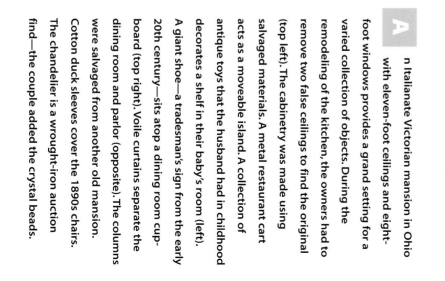

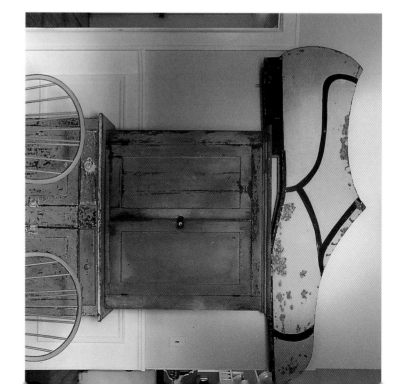

A n Italianate Victorian mansion in Ohio with eleven-foot ceilings and eight-foot windows provides a grand setting for a varied collection of objects. During the remodeling of the kitchen, the owners had to remove two false ceilings to find the original (top left). The cabinetry was made using salvaged materials. A metal restaurant cart acts as a moveable island. A collection of antique toys that the husband had in childhood decorates a shelf in their baby's room (left). A giant shoe—a tradesman's sign from the early 20th century—sits atop a dining room cup-board (top right). Voile curtains separate the dining room and parlor (opposite). The columns were salvaged from another old mansion. Cotton duck sleeves cover the 1890s chairs. The chandelier is a wrought-iron auction find—the couple added the crystal beads.

A suburban community center in Illinois proves that development houses need not be featureless. Broad rattan wing chairs and a cotton rug lend gracious informality to the living room (left). The look and colors of vintage textiles are recalled in both rug and fabrics. Slim-lined and armless, the dining chairs (top right) offer comfort in a tight space and invite lingering. In both the living and dining rooms, wood blinds cover the large windows, allowing for abundant light and privacy while drawing attention to the furnishings. Quiet neutral colors make the bedroom a restful spot (bottom right). The upholstered footboard and headboard echo the dining room chairs; sheer roman shades on the windows filter light beautifully.

The SOUTH

THE SOUTH HAS ALWAYS been a complicated place, and its homes illustrate just how heterogeneous—and deeply fascinating—it remains. A Mississippi log house, constructed from pre–Civil War dwellings; a newly linked pair of 19th-century cabins in Kentucky; a Federal period row house in Old Town Alexandria, Virginia; and a historic Florida cottage made from cypress and coral—are all revitalized with modern touches and yet still pay tribute to their Southern past.

T wo deteriorating pre–Civil War log cabins were reincarnated as this 10-room log home in central Mississippi. History means much to the couple who owns the cabin—they dine with the same pewter cutlery (with deer-antler handles) that the wife's family has used for three generations. They set their early 1800s dining table with mid-19th-century yellow-ware, and decorate the antique pine shelf in their kitchen with pantry boxes (opposite). A mid-1800s table and plank-bottom chairs furnish the sunporch (above). An occasional alligator can be seen lurking about the 2,500-acre property.

T here used to be two main buildings on Cabin Creek Farm in Kentucky: Hannah and Art Stearns's shop (a 100-year-old building) and their home, an 1863 poplar log cabin 50 feet away. Tired of shuttling back and forth, they designed a link between the two cabins. The couple collected aged doors, antique timbers, and old white furniture to make the new section appear as aged as the two structures it joins. Cabin Creek is famous for its signboards; two of their best-sellers hang in the kitchen (above). To create an old-barn feeling, Art installed old rugged beams. White-washed walls and a yellow floor transformed the keeping room (right). One beam had never been stained and was left untouched for posterity.

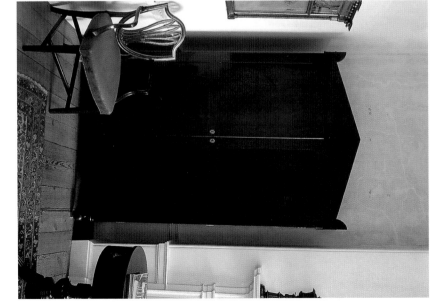

"I am a purist when it comes to restoration," states the owner of a 1795 row house in Alexandria, Virginia. He has filled his restoration project with fine regional antiques of the period. A carved tester bed from Virginia replete with its original hardware stars in the bedroom (top left). The mahogany armoire (above) by Alexandria furniture maker William Muir dates to about 1825. A free-standing tub, dated 1922, dominates the bathroom (bottom left), which is outfitted with a 19th-century fancy chair. In the second-floor parlor (opposite), the plastering remains unpainted. A rare circa 1825 marble-top center table stands beneath a French lighting fixture of the same period. Blue fabric turns a circa 1820 Baltimore sofa into an eye-catcher.

A Cape Cod HOUSE

I n the front hall (opposite), the bare essentials have taken on a kind of beauty. The floors are gleaming oak and the exposed staircase has been stripped to its bare-bones: treads, risers, and rail. The ceiling boasts beams that were rescued from an old house. Constructed from timber frames that were salvaged from four separate structures, the shingle-and-clapboard dwelling (above) is loosely based on rambling New England farmhouses of the 18th century. The telescoping design makes the 2,500-square-foot structure look bigger than it is.

EVER SINCE THE 17TH century, when the Pilgrims first created it, the sturdy house known as the Cape Cod has endured. Historical sources credit Yale president Timothy Dwight for coining the name in 1800. On a visit to Cape Cod, Dwight noted that nearly all the homes were similar: one-and-a-half stories high, with central chimneys, small windows, and gabled roofs. He called them "Cape Cod houses," and the name stuck.

The compactness and plainness of the Cape Cod design reflected a puritanical abhorrence for showiness of any kind. One Bostonian wrote, "There is…a remarkable republican simplicity in the style of buildings; little distinction that betokens wealth, an equality that extends to everything."

A new house in the Connecticut River Valley continues in that spirit. Built around an early 20th-century post-and-beam frame, the house shuns superficial ornamentation both inside and out. The facade features six-over-six paned windows, while the rear takes advantage of the river views with banks of sliding glass doors and windows. Despite the lack of frills, the house is infused with character, thanks to the many salvaged pieces used to build it.

G eorgia pine timbers salvaged from a circa 1910 silk mill in Lancaster, Pennsylvania, were recycled to construct the dwelling's stunning exposed framing. These powerful beams dominate the living room. A brick fireplace surround separates the living room from the entrance hall. Hand formed in wooden molds and kiln fired, the oversize Colonial-style bricks used to construct the wall were custom made in North Carolina.

A new soapstone wood-burning stove is as beautiful as it is functional in the family room (top left), which is open to both kitchen and dining room. Clock-maker Edward H. Stone of Maryland made the curly maple "coffin" wall clock, a reproduction of an 1810 timepiece. Inspired by Shaker case pieces, the kitchen's two-tone painted birch cabinetry includes freestanding china cupboards (bottom left). The early-20th-century ribbed glass lamps above the island were salvaged from a commercial building. A sliding glass center panel, engineered much like a pocket door, is all that separates the dining/family room from the outdoors (opposite). Windsor side chairs and a painted bench provide informal seating around the expandable cherry dining table.

A Salt BOX

WHEN THIS RHODE ISLAND couple set about to build an "Early American"-style house, they turned to the classic Saltbox, so called because the shape of the house resembled a Medieval saltbox. In the 1600s, few houses were built as Saltboxes. The lean-to in the back, which created the distinctive shape, was usually an addition.

For the wife, this home was a dream long in the making. She had been collecting pages from *Country Living* for years and knew exactly what she wanted. When she and her husband were ready to flesh out the bare interior of their newly constructed home, she went through the house nailing pictures to the exposed two-by-fours, illustrating the look she wanted in each room. Her husband, an electrical contractor by trade and a cabinetmaker by avocation, crafted many of the home's interior details, including molding, cabinetry, mantels, and even furniture. Over the years, they have completed the look with collections of antique pottery, textiles, and furnishings.

A s befits the Colonial period which inspired it, the house is gracefully simple (above). No shutters detract from the paned windows, and a large central chimney anchors the house. The owner's cabinetry-making skills can be seen in the dining room's pine corner cupboard (opposite). He stained it to match the reproduction tavern table and Windsor chairs. In striving for a Colonial air, the owners left the beams exposed, painted the woodwork the muted green that would, in an old house, have come over time, and treated the windows to plain muslin tab curtains.

o be truly authentic, the house had to have a keeping room (opposite). Here, the owners dry herbs from their garden on the exposed oak beams. Stones salvaged from an 18th-century house lend the hearth a genuine period look. The homeowner crafted both the harvest table and the slant-back cupboard, which now houses a collection of turn-of-the-century yellowware. An early American homespun and a mid-19th-century coverlet dress the late-19th-century rope beds in a small bedroom (above) on the third floor of the house. The circa 1880 desk to the left of the window was made in upstate New York. The trunk at the foot of the low-post bed was a boyhood possession of the father of one of the owners.

The Revolt of Mother, Mary Wilkins Freeman tells a tale of a woman who gets so angry at her farmer-husband for spending all of their money on a new barn that she takes up residence there. At the time, the idea of living in a barn was unthinkable. But today, our sense of what makes a home has changed, and our desire to preserve any piece of the past we can seems to know no bounds. Rather than lose barns, garages, carriage houses, or former factories to the wrecking ball, people are rescuing them and reincarnating them as dwellings.

Old houses in particular are benefiting from renewed attention. Some homeowners undertake historically authentic restorations, filling their spaces with period pieces; others favor a more creative approach, combining original architecture with the modern embellishments they love. ■

Design RECONSIDE

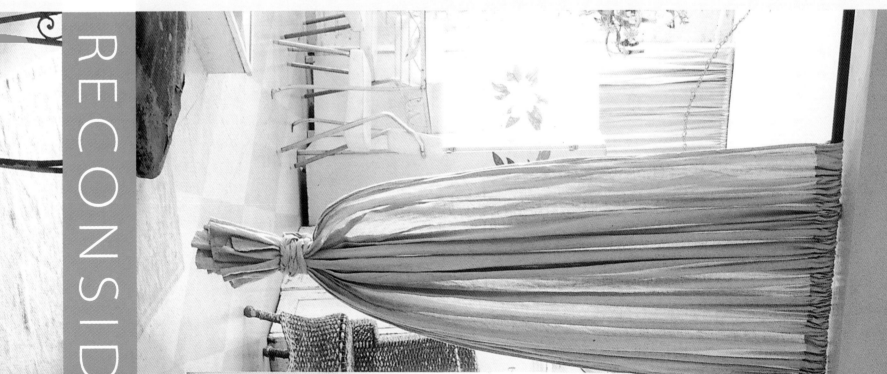

ERED

Home CONVERSIONS

THERE ARE TWO WAYS of treating a home that once was something else. The first is to disguise the past and create something altogether new. The second is to retain references to a home's earlier incarnation and even celebrate them. The woman who renovated a New York City loft followed the first approach, while two separate owners of barns took the second. All have succeeded in creating unique homes.

To evoke an ethereal mood in her New York City loft, the owner filled it with flea market finds and filmy fabric. She rescued the gothic arch in the living room (opposite) from a church in her Ohio hometown. A Victorian drapery panel dresses the daybed. A Hoosier cabinet top and Ohio relics such as a gym light fixture and a factory window outfit the kitchen (above left). Downtown breezes blow through the bathroom, where a faux-tile paint treatment covers up the once carpeted floor (above right).

Several years ago, a Manhattan loft-dweller stared at her black plastered walls and industrial carpeting and decided it was time for a change. She exposed the apartment's original brick walls and wood flooring, then coated the walls in milky white paint and gathered lengths of diaphanous linen for the windows and for curtains between rooms.

The goal of the owner of a Long Island barn was to maintain the integrity of the structure's late 18th-century frame. To do so, he housed bedrooms and bathrooms in new additions so that the original building could serve as an undivided great room, incorporating the living, dining, and cooking areas.

reating a sense of discrete spaces can be tricky in a loft. The owner divided up her square-footage with partial walls, filmy linen draperies, and furnishings—such as a decoupage screen, which separates the eating and cooking areas. For continuity she painted a harlequin-patterned floor, uniting the rooms in the commodious loft.

The glass-topped table was part of a vintage outdoor-furniture set. White vinyl chairs from the 1960s serve as comfy and informal dining chairs. Virtually all the furnishings in the home are salvaged pieces, most with their original paint. The owner's motto is simple: The more peeling paint, the better. It shows that a piece has lived.

To expose the barn's hand-hewn oak skeleton, he installed new white pine interior siding around it.

The owners of another barn on Long Island share the first owner's philosophy. They let the 19th-century barn itself dictate the direction of the project. The layout remains relatively unchanged from the original design, with a loft at either end and a central breezeway with rows of glass doors and windows replacing the traditional barn doors. Many of the unpretentious objects that decorate the barn, including farm tools and a dilapidated horse-drawn carriage, would be equally at home on a real farm. The owners even enclosed one of the lofts with netting so that the swallows could remain.

"Barns tend to be dark, so our design needed to bring in as much sunlight as possible," says the man who lives in a light-filled 200-year-old New Jersey barn, which he moved to Long Island, New York. Three pine boards from a late-19th-century barn were transformed into a massive 15-foot dining table (opposite). Remnants from a late-19th-century wrought-iron fence form the base. New red cedar shingles sheathe the original structure (top right), situated on one and a half acres. Across the kitchen ceiling, beams indicate the original divisions between the barn's stalls (right).

G uests of all ages love the bunk room in one of the barn's new additions (above). The owner installed authentic vintage radiators that he had sandblasted and repainted because they triggered fond memories of his childhood home. A freestanding fireplace functions as the focal point of the main living area and helps delineate dining and living rooms (right). The fireplace was placed here so that it would not obstruct the barn frame. Mismatched furnishings gathered during trips to flea markets give the interior a relaxed and accommodating atmosphere. "I chose materials that could take a beating," says the owner: old wood, wrought iron, stainless steel and canvas slipcovers.

W hen remodeling a circa 1869 barn, the two men who own it kept plenty of reminders of the structure's past life. Simple battens are part of those reminders, but new elements are also deliberately barn-like, such as the Dutch exterior doors (top left). The pair also layered their home with character-infused antiques such as the pie safe from the 1800s with pierced tin door fronts. The original hayloft forms the ceiling for one of the bedrooms (left). In the loft, the two store a carriage for their neighbor, whose family once owned the farmstead. The blue chest at the foot of the tester bed is a 19th-century reproduction of an Amish Bible box. Many of the pieces in the barn predate it. A pine cupboard (opposite) from Pennsylvania, made between 1820 and 1850, holds early-19th-century Staffordshire lusterware. The banister-back chair dates to the mid-1700s and wears at least four layers of paint.

Home RENOVATIONS

TO RESTORE AN OLD structure—and make it livable—takes vision, patience, and often, a large budget. Perseverance is key; renovations can stretch out over decades. "In 36 years we have never stopped working on the place," laments the owner of an 18th-century Pennsylvania home. But what a restoration requires most of all is a passion for the character of the old house. It also takes the ability to see through old changes that detract from the home's original spirit, and the imagination to make

F ifty-five windows grace the century-old Queen Anne-style home (above); many of which look out onto Long Island Sound. A trompe l'oeil rug decorates the dining room's oak floor (opposite). The owner painted the flowers freehand, using blossoms from her garden as models. Four coats of polyurethane protect it. The ornately carved marble-topped buffet was in the house when the owners moved in; they believe it was made for the room.

a relic from the past function for modern life. "Our house can be a slave driver," says the owner of a rambling Victorian, "but we love it nonetheless."

Each of the houses is different—a seaside Victorian replete with a turret and wide porches; an 1870 farmhouse made over in the Greek Revival style; an elegant Pennsylvania stone dwelling that was first built in 1740; and a 200-year-old Vermont farmhouse restored with attention both to historical accuracy and health concerns. They all have one thing in common: owners who look on the renovation of their homes as nothing less than an act of love.

The original glazed fireplace tiles in the living room (opposite) dictated the room's color scheme. Against the tropical blue walls, a vintage quilt provides graphic drama. Elaborate woodwork adorns the house, particularly in the stairwell (top right). The detailing was first painted in the 1930s, and repeats the bead-and-panel pattern seen in all the rooms. Hidden in a third-floor room when the family bought the house in 1978, the twin iron beds (bottom right) weigh a ton, according to one of the owners. Instead of restoring the painted finish, she simply chipped away a little more paint to accentuate the patina (right).

he grand columns and porches notwithstanding, this home (above) was a plain-Jane 1870 farmhouse until an architect—a great fan of Greek Revival style—undertook its renovation. Going against the historical formula that called for important rooms to be at the front, the architect positioned the living room and master bedroom at the rear of the house, which gave them more privacy and better views. Rescued from a house that was demolished, an early-19th-century mantel serves as a model for the detailing on the coffered ceiling, built-in bookcases, and overmantel in the living room (right). The wide chestnut floorboards were discovered in the house's attic. A Hudson River School landscape hangs above the mantel.

he family that owns an old Pennsylvania farmhouse (the original structure dates from 1740, with additions in 1840, 1929, and 1991) has taken care to decorate it in a manner that befits its history, with fine Philadelphia-area antiques from the early 1800s. Brilliant yellow walls and 19th-century Canton porcelain distinguish the dining room (opposite), which is furnished with a circa 1815 table, a circa 1740 walnut Queen Anne highboy, and circa 1810 side chairs and armchairs made by Joseph B. Barry, a celebrated Philadelphia cabinetmaker. In the foreground, a copper urn rests atop a circa 1810 lyre-base worktable. Situated in the oldest section of the house, the living room (above) is formally appointed with 19th-century Philadelphia antiques, including a graceful circa 1810 sofa featuring carved feathers on its crest rail and a circa 1810 card table with brass accents. Both pieces have been attributed to Joseph B. Barry.

A Federal FARMHOUSE

AT FIRST, THE 1792 FARMHOUSE on 55 acres of land in Vermont seemed like a dream come true to the husband and wife who bought it. She had always hankered after an old house; he had long dreamed of having land. As time passed, however, the wife realized that she was getting sick fairly regularly and that her allergies were especially bothersome whenever she spent a lot of time in the house.

After hiring an environmental engineer, the couple discovered that the damp, inadequately insulated dwelling was plagued by 200 years worth of mold and mildew. To remedy the problem, the pair set out to make their house healthy as well as to restore it. In addition to disinfecting the entire structure and installing custom-made thermal windows with vintage glass, they brought wiring up to code and installed cotton insulation instead of the usual fiberglass. They also removed all lead-based paint and then finished walls, floors, and woodwork with all-natural paints, sealers, and stains.

ocated on a quiet road in rural Vermont, the three-bedroom clapboard house (above) features a classic Federal-style center chimney and an entrance with transom and sidelights. During the renovation, the dining room's plaster ceiling was removed to expose its original beams (opposite). Save for a tasseled swag at the window, the room is virtually fabric-free so as to cut down on dust and other allergy-provoking substances. The almost stark decor suits the old farmhouse well; the absence of pattern makes the architecture and the lines of the country antiques stand out.

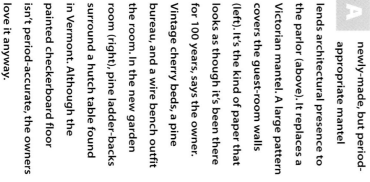

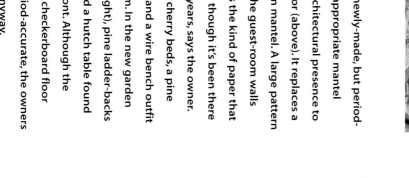

A newly-made, but period-appropriate mantel lends architectural presence to the parlor (above). It replaces a Victorian mantel. A large pattern covers the guest-room walls (left). It's the kind of paper that looks as though it's been there for 100 years, says the owner. Vintage cherry beds, a pine bureau, and a wire bench outfit the room. In the new garden room (right), pine ladder-backs surround a hutch table found in Vermont. Although the painted checkerboard floor isn't period-accurate, the owners love it anyway.

FOR A CHILD, AN OUTDOOR PLAY-house is sheer heaven—a special, secret place unbounded by rules, where imaginations can soar. Grown-ups as well take delight in a tiny building where they have to bend their heads to enter, where no one

New Spaces

thinks to look for them and real life recedes.

Such a sanctuary can take many forms—it can be a newly built guest cottage, a conservatory, or a writer's studio. Or it can be a musty shed that has been cleaned up and recast in a new role—as a gardener's getaway perhaps, or a painter's atelier.

Such a spot offers an opportunity to let the imagination soar. Homeowners can exercise their creativity by painting it daring shades, while decorating it with welcoming furnishings and homey touches and filling it with objects they love make it a true home away from home. ■

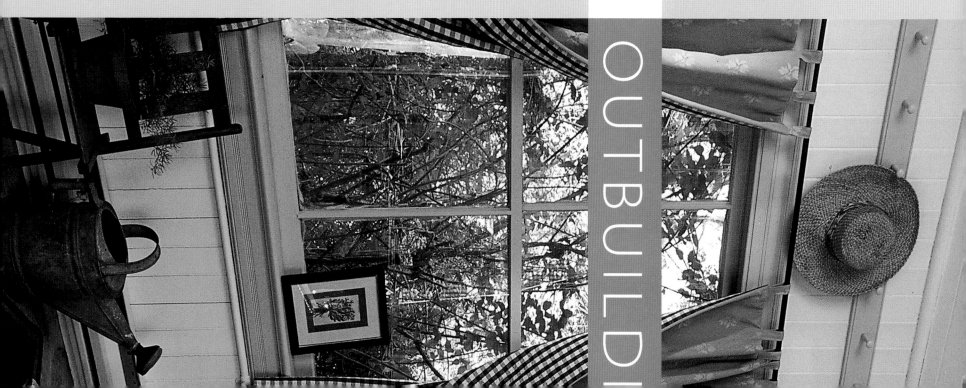

OUTBUILD

Existing STRUCTURES

IN THE SOUTH, outbuildings on a farm were known, quaintly enough, as dependencies. These extra buildings were dependent on the main house for necessities, but were separate entities, like children around a mother's skirt. Such additional buildings are fun to make over and even more fun to use. Often, they are very easily transformed—with a fresh coat of paint, a new floor, a clearing away of overgrown bushes, trees, and weeds—into spaces that are both intimate and inspiring.

A storage shed, blessed with a high-pitched ceiling and fieldstone fireplace, became a welcoming gardener's retreat when the owners widened the front stoop and added window boxes and a stone path (above right). A closet now functions as the potting area (above left). Deep enough for filling watering cans, the original soapstone sink has generous work space (opposite). The shower is handy for cleaning up after a good day's work in the dirt.

n a previous life, a minute retreat (opposite) on an old Maryland farm was a washhouse. Creative decorating brings the 12-by-12-foot space to life as a warm-weather hideaway. Old scythes and baskets look like sculpture against whitewashed walls. A garland of dried lemon leaves and lilies festoons the fireplace, a salvaged Federal-style pediment adorns the wall, and buckets of freshly-cut blooms fill the air with scent. A homespun cotton dress makes a decorative statement when hung on a wall (above left). Summer flowers gathered in buckets create a seasonal mood in the cabin, where in good weather the door and windows are always open. The old brick floor helps keep the space cool (above right). Furnishings and walls were white-washed with watered-down latex paint for a crisp look.

New STRUCTURES

MANY LOTS HAVE THE yard space for an additional small dwelling if one does not already exist. Constructing an outbuilding from scratch allows homeowners to indulge their wishes—and sometimes their fantasies. There are no rules to be followed, and the level of luxury these spaces achieve becomes a personal decision. Some consider electricity and running water unnecessary amenities in such spaces, creating workshops, fishing huts, conservatories, or potting sheds that are modest, but always

A 1920s picket fence from New England lends presence to an 8-by-20-foot mail-order greenhouse in Maryland (above). Built of translucent Mylar framed in aluminum, the structure provides state-of-the-art growing conditions for young myrtles and ivy (opposite). Full-grown topiaries stand tall against a salvaged fanlight. Heated with propane, the greenhouse maintains a controlled temperature.

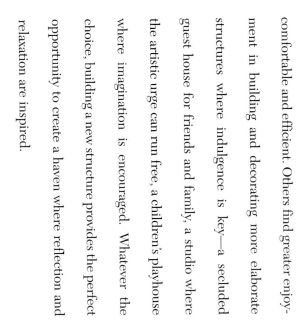

comfortable and efficient. Others find greater enjoyment in building and decorating more elaborate structures where indulgence is key—a secluded guest house for friends and family, a studio where the artistic urge can run free, a children's playhouse where imagination is encouraged. Whatever the choice, building a new structure provides the perfect opportunity to create a haven where reflection and relaxation are inspired.

"W hen I'm in there I feel like I'm seven years old," says one of the owners of the two-room cabin that they built on their wooded property. Salvaged oversized windows in the cabin's smaller room (it measures 8-by-8) provide unrestricted forest views and ample daylight (top left). In the miniature alcove kitchen of sorts (bottom left), the couple installed as many shelves as possible for storage. Because the cabin lacks running water, meals here are simple affairs. Like a Pullman berth, the cupboard bed epitomizes coziness (opposite). A checked tablecloth became the spread; three cotton dish towels were transformed into cheerful pillowcases. A rescued sidelight used horizontally provides the bunk with a window of its own.

Two fishing buddies, Craig Bero and Mike Thielke, built an angling hut/fishing cabin by hand on an island in the waters of Little Bear Creek in upstate New York. It has become a nature retreat both for them and for the kids who attend Craig's fishing camp, called The Clearing. They furnished it with rustic antiques and everything necessary for a weekend with rod and reel. A local blacksmith forged the door's cast-iron trout hinges and feathered-salmon fly latch (left). The fishing tackle sign is from a bait shop Craig patronized as a boy. Birch slabs that cover the walls (opposite) once chinked a long cabin near Craig's boyhood home in Wisconsin. Potawatomi artisans berry-painted the speckled trout on the paddle above the doorway. As a boy, Craig cleaned fish on the split-ash table.

The charms of Victorian style are captured in a diminutive hideaway (above) constructed by a loving grandfather out of recycled materials. A Dutch door and cupboards help little imaginations in the pretend kitchen (top left). To achieve the look of bull's-eye molding on the door and window frames, the owner cut squares of wood, then glued wooden toy wheels in the center of them. A bean bag invites curling up in a corner where painted crates house a juvenile library (bottom left). An abandoned cupboard was recycled to create the beadboard wainscoting. For safety, the owner used Plexiglas instead of glass in most of the windows and auto-detailing tape to create the illusion of panes. No grown-ups are allowed in the snug loft (opposite), which features an air mattress dressed with a vintage chenille pillow and cotton bed linens. A picnic basket serves as a bedside table.

The

PART TWO

Spirit of COUNTRY

for the staying power of country style is its refreshing informality. No stiff fabrics, no draperies with tight pleats, no high-gloss finishes. Certainly it's hard to be formal in a room where peeling paint on an object is prized. But living amongst rustic furnishings doesn't mean watching television in a ladderback chair. More and more, country has come to mean real comfort. Sofas and upholstered chairs are slouchy and soft—the kind you can sink into. Fabrics help keep the look easy—mattress ticking, cotton duck, and even on the right piece, super-soft velvet. But comfort can go beyond cushioning. It

Easy Country

NEW COMF

can come from cooking in a well-organized space blessed with ample light, soaking in a deep old tub; putting up your feet in a room bathed in light, or simply climbing into a bed that cradles you. ■

Easy LIVING

A WEEKEND HOME IS supposed to be fuss-free. After all, who wants to worry about cleaning on their time off? A restful spot is what designer Peri Wolfman desired of her newly constructed weekend house on Long Island's shore. To her, restful means simplicity. There is no pattern and only pale colors in the house, except for the worn hues of rustic folk painted pieces. "I don't like spots of color," she explains, "and I have a very hectic life and like my surroundings to be serene." Another reason for the lack of color (and window treatments) was to shift the focus onto the idyllic outdoors. "I wanted the outside to be important," she says, "and to be always looking out." The unpretentious vintage furnishings have clean lines and chipped paint—even new items, such as mirrored medicine cabinets in the master bathroom, were custom made to resemble antique mirrors. Her criteria for upholstered pieces were straightforward: comfortable, simple, and washable. The plump furnishings keep the uncluttered decor from looking too bare bones.

A lthough the house is newly built, owner Peri Wolfman filled it with plenty of character-imbuing accents such as a vintage table with original paint and the staircase's newel-post, which she discovered at a local antiques show (opposite). White and yellow in all their permutations form an enduring palette for the weekend house. "I wanted a look that was spare but not austere," says Wolfman. In the living room (above), loose slipcovers on fat easy chairs keep the decorating on the informal side. They slip off easily for cleaning.

he bygone touches of the master bathroom (top left) include a cast-iron bathtub and a cutout crescent moon in the door—a humorous reference to old-time outhouses. A half-door in the laundry room (above) opens to reveal a tiny storage space. Wolfman tucked many such spaces into the home to enforce the idea of an old house. A bed crafted from salvaged architectural artifacts and dressed in antique linens presides over the master bedroom (bottom left). An example of creative recycling: Old barn hooks serve as curtain rods on the long windows. A mid-1800 marble-topped French baker's table takes on a new life as a work island in the kitchen (opposite). For a true farmhouse feel, the kitchen's ceiling is deliberately two feet lower than the dining room's.

Great LIVING AREAS

WHAT MAKES A wonderful living or family room? The answer lies not in filling a space with beautiful fabrics and antiques, but in creating comfort. The homes on these pages have one thing in common—a total lack of pretense. The homeowners were not trying to create showplaces, but spaces where someone could put their feet up on the coffee table, lie down on the sofa, curl up in a big chair, and where children can play. Many are weekend houses, which helps explain the lack of accessories and the slouchy slipcovers. They are places where people want to be outside hiking or lying in the hammock, or inside absorbed in a mystery novel, not worrying about whether the porcelain is dusted. They are owned by people who love their houses and their decorating, but who don't want that to intrude on having fun. "My goal was to create a comfortable, relaxed home in harmony with its surroundings," explains the owner of a North Carolina weekend getaway house. "Its simplicity makes it easy to maintain and a lot safer for the little children who visit us here."

reating cozy corners can be a challenge in a space unbroken by walls, but a New Jersey homeowner has done it in her 150-year-old barn-turned-house (opposite). Beside the stairwell, a fat, single-armed chair, draped in a casual slipcover, nestles beside a seven-drawer cherry chest from the Shaker community in New Lebanon, New York. Friendly, informal furnishings also characterize a Maine Victorian. In the living room (above), twin wicker armchairs flank the new beadboard cabinet, which holds a television and VCR.

"I wanted this place to feel airy, like a little tree house," says the landscape painter and art teacher who lives in a small apartment, along with her husband and son, in a landmark building in Denver. Though the flat is diminutive, it lives large thanks to sky blue walls in the living room and sun room, white-washed wood floors and large windows left bare to take advantage of the views. The limited number of furnishings are upholstered in pale shades and all are slim in line. "Because the apartment is small, using less made it seem more spacious," she says. The owner inherited the down-filled sofa from her grandmother; her great-grandparents brought the low-slung coffee table home with them after a 1910 trip to Morocco.

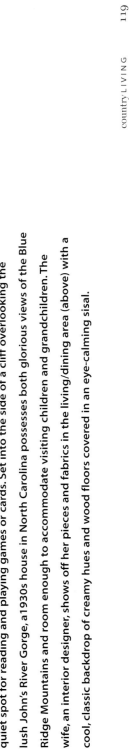

F loor-to-ceiling bookshelves bring old-world warmth to a Tudor-style great room (opposite) in a 1914 Connecticut house. The owners divvied up the large room into activity centers to make it more useful. The bookshelves and vintage gaming table turn a corner into a quiet spot for reading and playing games or cards. Set into the side of a cliff overlooking the lush John's River Gorge, a 1930s house in North Carolina possesses both glorious views of the Blue Ridge Mountains and room enough to accommodate visiting children and grandchildren. The wife, an interior designer, shows off her pieces and fabrics in the living/dining area (above) with a cool, classic backdrop of creamy hues and wood floors covered in an eye-calming sisal.

A hand-painted vine and oversized baskets help bring intimacy to a dining bay with a vaulted ceiling (top left). The many-windowed area is paved in tile for easy care. The new pedestal table is crafted of silver maple; the chairs recall the designs of Duncan Phyfe. Though the home is newly built, the architect imbued it with old-house details such as the plaster plaque above the hearth in the living room (left). Doors next to the built-in fireplace disguise the television. Vintage touches enliven another brand-new home (right). Exposed beams lend character to the family room, where loose-fitting, washable cotton slipcovers the amply cushioned seating. One set of aged shutters fills in for a window treatment; another serves as a decorative screen.

EVERYONE LOVES AN old house, but few love an old kitchen. Our way of living—particularly regarding the kitchen—has changed dramatically over the years. The demand is for welcoming, open kitchens that are highly practical and functional, and also work well for several cooks. Ample storage is also an important need, as well as space for dining and entertaining.

There lies the challenge for architects and kitchen designers: how to create a thoroughly modern space with state-of-the art appliances and layout that still has the warmth and character of an old house. As the kitchens on these pages illustrate, the secret lies in softening the high-tech necessities with the best of the past. Cabinetry echoes the look of built-in furniture, even down to knobs borrowed from bedroom dressers. Storage is a relaxed mix of open shelving, concealed space, and antique pieces. Texture-giving materials such as wide-plank pine floors, stone (or stone-like synthetic) or tile countertops, and exposed beams made from old wood offer contrast and create interest.

Big Family KITCHENS

V intage ingredients, such as marble-tile countertops, beadboard paneling, and a rebuilt 1913 stove, make a new kitchen (formerly a bedroom) appear timeless in a seaside Victorian (opposite). To delineate the kitchen and dining areas (above) in an 1830s whaler's house, the owner lined the appliances against one wall and used a low pine cupboard as a room divider. The sliver of window above the counter is an upturned transom. The mirror is a feng shui maneuver: its placement "means I never turn my back to the room," the owner explains.